Copyright (C) 2023 by Complete SET LLC.
All rights reserved under International and Pan-American Copyright Conventions.

Published by Complete SET.
Written by Tanner Simkins.
Cover by Tanner Simkins.

No part of this text may be reproduced, transmitted, downloaded, decompiled, sever-engineered, or stored in or introduced into any information storage and retrieval system, in any form or by any means, whether electronic or mechanical, now known or hereinafter invented, without the express written permission of author or the publisher,
Library of Congress Cataloging in-Publication data is available upon request.

ISBN 979-8-218-23009-8

Dedicated to Caitlin, Sienna, and Stella for their love and support

*An Abbreviated Compendium
for Navigating the NCAA
Name, Image, and Likeness Landscape*

TANNER SIMKINS

I. Overview

- Brief summary of the Name, Image, and Likeness (NIL) topic
- Importance of the NIL changes to the NCAA landscape

II. History of NIL in NCAA

- Early days of NCAA: Athletes as amateurs
- Evolution of athlete rights and the rise of NIL discussions
- Key court cases and rulings
- Transition towards supporting NIL rights

III. NCAA Regulations

- Overview of NCAA's NIL policy
- Detailed review of what student-athletes can and can't do under the new policy
- Role of the NCAA in monitoring and enforcement

IV. State Laws

- The role of state laws in forcing the NCAA's hand on NIL
- Differences in state laws
- How the NCAA is dealing with differing state laws
- The potential role of federal legislation to harmonize laws

V. University Regulations

- The autonomy of universities in creating their own NIL policies
- Examples of university-specific rules
- Role of universities in NIL education and compliance

VI. NIL Deal Statistics

- Overview of the financial impact since the implementation of NIL
- Examples of major NIL deals and averages
- The effect of NIL deals on athlete income

VII. Impact on Different Sports

- Disparity between NIL opportunities in revenue-generating sports vs. other sports
- Impact on recruiting across different sports
- Gender differences in NIL opportunities

VIII. NIL Representatives, Sports Agents, and Ethical Considerations

- Interplay between student-athletes and representatives
- Ethical concerns

IX. Current Trends

- Rise of NIL collectives and pooled sponsorship deals
- Universities partnering with marketing companies for NIL opportunities
- Increase in entrepreneurial activities among athletes

X. Future Predictions

- Potential for federal legislation on NIL
- Predicted impact of NIL on the future of college sports
- Role of NIL in athletes' decisions to stay in school or go pro

XI. NIL and tax

- Overview on the NIL tax implications on student-athletes, collectives, and more

XII. Conclusion

- Recap of the changing NIL landscape
- The importance of understanding NIL for all stakeholders
- Final thoughts on the future of NIL in NCAA

I. Overview

The landscape of collegiate athletics has undergone a transformational shift with the introduction of Name, Image, and Likeness (NIL) rights for NCAA student-athletes. The core purpose of this white paper is to provide a comprehensive overview of the mechanics of NIL, its genesis, regulations at various levels, economic impact, and the broader implications it holds for the future of collegiate sports.

Historically, NCAA athletes were deemed amateurs, a distinction that prohibited them from profiting from their sporting prowess. With the recent evolution in NIL rights, a radical change has taken place. NCAA athletes can now monetize their personal brand while still retaining their eligibility, creating a seismic shift in the amateurism model that has underpinned collegiate sports for over a century.

This transformation has not been without its complexities. Different state laws, NCAA rules, and university regulations all intertwine in a complex tapestry of governance. This paper dissects these elements to provide a clear understanding of the NIL landscape.

The implementation of NIL rights has also introduced a new economic dynamic into collegiate sports. Student-athletes have started to harness the power of their personal brands, signing endorsement deals that were once off-limits. This new income source has significant implications for the students themselves, the universities they attend, and the businesses and brands that engage with them.

The introduction of NIL rights has had varying impacts across different sports. Revenue-generating sports such as football and basketball have seen significant activity, while athletes in non-revenue sports are carving out their own unique opportunities. The potential impact on gender equality and diversity within collegiate sports is also a crucial area of focus.

Looking ahead, current trends suggest that NIL will continue to shape the future of collegiate sports. The rise of collective deals, the importance of digital platforms, and the entrepreneurial spirit being displayed by student-athletes are all key indicators of where the landscape is heading.

The text concludes with a series of future predictions, drawing on the insights gathered to anticipate the trajectory of NIL in the NCAA landscape. The need for clear federal legislation, the ongoing impact on recruitment, and the potential for more student-athletes to consider staying in school are all topics of consideration.

The changes brought about by NIL rights are both thrilling and complex. This white paper aims to navigate these intricacies and provide a clear and comprehensive understanding of the NIL mechanics, its effects, and its potential trajectory. The dawn of this new era in collegiate sports holds immense promise, and understanding it will be crucial for all stakeholders involved.

II. History of NIL in NCAA

Since its establishment in 1906, the NCAA has embraced the principle of amateurism, prohibiting student-athletes from monetizing their sports-related activities. This principle has been integral to the collegiate sports model, maintaining a distinct boundary between amateur collegiate sports and professional leagues.

The issue of athletes' rights and their ability to profit from their Name, Image, and Likeness (NIL) started to gain traction in the late 20th and early 21st century. The discussion revolved around fairness and equity, as universities, coaches, and the NCAA reaped significant financial benefits from collegiate sports, while the athletes themselves, the primary value drivers, were restricted by the rules of amateurism.

Key court cases have played a pivotal role in the evolution of NIL rights. One of the most significant was the landmark case of O'Bannon v. NCAA in 2014. Ed O'Bannon, a former UCLA basketball player, challenged the NCAA's use of former student-athletes' images for commercial purposes without compensation. The court ruled in O'Bannon's favor, arguing that the NCAA's rules on compensation were an unlawful restraint of trade.

Despite this victory, the ruling did not directly lead to the establishment of NIL rights for student-athletes. The court suggested that colleges could put money into a trust for athletes to access post-graduation but stopped short of allowing athletes to profit from endorsements or their own merchandise while still in school.

The conversation around NIL rights gained momentum in the late 2010s. In 2019, California passed the Fair Pay to Play Act, becoming the first state to allow collegiate athletes to profit from their NIL. The legislation, set to take effect in 2023, posed a direct challenge to the NCAA's longstanding amateurism rules.

In response to these developments, the NCAA Board of Governors announced in October 2019 that it would begin the process of modifying its rules to allow athletes to profit from their NIL "in a manner consistent with the collegiate model."

The pressure on the NCAA was further escalated by other states enacting NIL legislation, many of which had laws set to take effect before California's. This patchwork of differing state laws posed a significant challenge to the NCAA's desire for consistent national rules.

Eventually, on July 1, 2021, the NCAA adopted a temporary policy permitting student-athletes to monetize their NIL, a monumental shift in the history of collegiate sports. This move didn't represent the NCAA's final word on NIL, but it was a significant step toward aligning the association's rules with the changing societal and legal perspectives on the matter.

In summary, the journey towards the recognition of NIL rights for NCAA athletes has been shaped by various forces. Legal challenges, state laws, and growing public sentiment for fairness have collectively compelled the NCAA to rewrite its longstanding principles of amateurism. This shift marks a new chapter in the NCAA's history, the effects of which are just beginning to unfold.

III. NCAA Regulations

On July 1, 2021, the NCAA adopted an interim policy that allows student-athletes to monetize their Name, Image, and Likeness (NIL), marking a significant departure from their previous regulations. Under the new policy, all NCAA divisions are required to consider any NIL rules as null, thereby allowing athletes to participate in NIL activities without losing their eligibility.

The NCAA's interim NIL policy includes several key provisions:
1. Individual Rights: Athletes are permitted to profit from their NIL. This includes participating in advertisements, selling merchandise, or conducting camps and clinics, among other activities. Athletes can also hire agents or other representatives to manage NIL opportunities.
2. Institutional Involvement: While universities can educate their student-athletes about NIL, they cannot directly or indirectly compensate their athletes for NIL activities. Additionally, schools are barred from using NIL as a recruiting incentive.
3. Reporting: Student-athletes are expected to report their NIL activities, as required by their respective institution or conference.

It's important to note that the NCAA's interim policy primarily serves as a placeholder until a more permanent solution is established. The NCAA still maintains its commitment to creating a national standard for NIL, with the hope of preventing discrepancies across different states.

One of the primary responsibilities of the NCAA under this new policy is monitoring and enforcement. Although the NCAA no longer prohibits NIL activities, there are still rules in place to ensure fair competition. For example, athletes cannot use their NIL for pay-for-play, impermissible benefits, or recruiting inducements. Furthermore, the NCAA retains its authority to penalize schools or athletes who violate these rules.

The NCAA's interim NIL policy represents a substantial shift in the association's traditional stance on amateurism. However, the policy is not without its complexities and uncertainties. As the NCAA continues to navigate this new landscape, it remains to be seen how these regulations will evolve to balance the interests of student-athletes, institutions, and the integrity of collegiate sports.

IV. State Laws

State laws have played a pivotal role in advancing the Name, Image, and Likeness (NIL) rights for NCAA athletes. While the NCAA was hesitant to reform its regulations, various states moved forward with legislation that allowed their student-athletes to profit from their NIL, essentially forcing the NCAA's hand.

> 1. California's Fair Pay to Play Act: Signed into law in 2019 and set to take effect in 2023, this was the first legislation that permitted student-athletes to profit from their NIL. It prohibits California universities from denying athletes the opportunity to earn compensation for the use of their NIL or revoke scholarships from athletes who do so.
> 2. Florida's Intercollegiate Athlete Compensation and Rights Bill: This law, effective from July 1, 2021, allows student-athletes in Florida to earn compensation for their NIL and hire a licensed agent. Importantly, it also prohibits universities and athletic associations from preventing athletes from such opportunities.
> 3. Colorado's Senate Bill 20-123: Effective from January 1, 2023, this legislation allows Colorado student-athletes to earn compensation from their NIL and sign endorsement deals. It also mandates financial literacy and life skills workshops for student-athletes.

Several other states, including Nebraska, New Jersey, Alabama, Mississippi, and Georgia, also passed similar NIL laws that were scheduled to take effect on or before July 1, 2021. As a result, the NCAA had to adjust its policy to maintain a level playing field for student-athletes in different states.

Notably, each state's law varies slightly in its requirements and restrictions, creating a patchwork of rules across the country. Some laws, for instance, prevent athletes from signing deals that conflict with their school's existing contracts, while others prohibit certain types of endorsements, such as those promoting gambling or alcohol.

These state laws also place different requirements on universities. Some require schools to provide financial literacy training, while others mandate health and disability insurance.

The variances in state laws pose a significant challenge for the NCAA, which traditionally prided itself on maintaining uniform rules across the country. The patchwork of state laws has underscored the need for federal legislation to establish a national standard for NIL, an effort the NCAA has actively been advocating for in the U.S. Congress.

V. University Regulations

Alongside NCAA and state regulations, universities themselves have played a significant role in shaping the Name, Image, and Likeness (NIL) landscape. Each university has the autonomy to devise its own policies within the broader confines of state laws and NCAA rules.

Education and Guidance: Many universities have developed educational programs to guide student-athletes through the complexities of NIL. They offer resources and tools that help athletes understand the rules, manage potential contracts, and ensure compliance with NCAA and state regulations. Some institutions have even partnered with third-party companies that specialize in NIL education, contract management, and financial literacy.

Monitoring and Compliance: Universities are also responsible for establishing a system to monitor and maintain compliance with NIL policies. In some cases, student-athletes are required to disclose their NIL activities and contracts to their institution. The university is then responsible for ensuring these activities are in compliance with state and NCAA rules.

Restrictions: While NIL policies have granted athletes new opportunities, universities still have a say in what types of activities are permitted. Some institutions have enacted additional restrictions on the types of endorsements student-athletes can accept, such as prohibiting partnerships that could damage the school's reputation. Additionally, many universities prohibit activities that would conflict with institutional contracts, such as an athlete endorsing a different athletic apparel company than the university's sponsor.

Institution-Specific Examples:
- The University of Miami has been proactive in the NIL space, leveraging its location in a major city with strong corporate ties. The university has engaged INFLCR, a company that assists in athlete brand building and NIL deal compliance.
- Ohio State University has developed an extensive NIL program called "THE Platform," designed to support student-athletes in maximizing their NIL potential. The program offers education on brand building, financial management, and entrepreneurship.

While universities are not allowed to directly pay athletes or orchestrate NIL deals, they play an essential role in guiding, supporting, and monitoring their student-athletes in this new landscape. Each university's approach to NIL can impact their attractiveness to prospective student-athletes, making it an important factor in the competitive world of collegiate sports recruiting. As NIL continues to evolve, the university's role in shaping its implementation and impact will remain crucial.

VI. Economic Statistics

The advent of Name, Image, and Likeness (NIL) rights has unlocked a new economic frontier for NCAA student-athletes. From endorsement deals and social media monetization to entrepreneurship and private lessons, athletes now have numerous avenues to generate income from their personal brand. While the NIL marketplace is still in its infancy and comprehensive data is limited, early statistics indicate the significant potential value that this market holds.

> 1. General Earnings: Within just a month of the NIL rules taking effect, student-athletes had already made millions of dollars, according to various reports. Athletes in high-profile sports such as football and basketball have signed deals worth tens of thousands, and in some cases, hundreds of thousands of dollars.
> 2. Social Media Monetization: Given the sizable social media followings that many student-athletes possess, monetizing these platforms has been a significant focus of NIL activities. Opendorse, a company that assists athletes with NIL opportunities, estimates that top-tier student-athletes could generate six-figure incomes annually from social media endorsements alone.
> 3. Diverse Opportunities: Despite the dominance of football and men's basketball, student-athletes from a variety of sports have capitalized on NIL opportunities. Gymnasts, track and field athletes, and swimmers, among others, have secured endorsement deals and monetized their social media platforms.
> 4. Geographic Differences: The potential NIL earnings vary significantly across the country, primarily driven by differences in fan base size and local economic conditions. A study from the Athletic Director U and Navigate Research estimated that student-athletes at schools in major conferences could earn between $600 and $1600 annually on average, with significant variability based on the sport, individual performance, and marketability.
> 5. Women's Sports: Women's sports have demonstrated strong potential in the NIL marketplace. Icon Source, a digital marketplace for endorsement deals, noted that in the first month of NIL, nearly half of the deals executed on their platform involved female athletes.

These statistics highlight the significant potential that NIL rights present for NCAA student-athletes. However, the economic landscape of NIL is still evolving, and it's yet to be seen how these opportunities will shape the financial prospects of student-athletes in the long term. The disparity in earning potential between different sports, genders, and regions is an important area of focus as the NIL era unfolds.

VII. Impact on Different Sports

The new Name, Image, and Likeness (NIL) policies have broad implications across all collegiate sports, though the impact is not uniform. While every NCAA athlete now has the opportunity to monetize their NIL, the marketability and earning potential vary significantly across different sports.

High-Profile Sports: Football and Men's Basketball
As the most visible and popular collegiate sports, football and men's basketball have been at the forefront of the NIL conversation. Players in these sports often have significant followings and high levels of exposure, making them attractive to businesses for endorsements and promotional opportunities. High-profile athletes in these sports have signed some of the most lucrative deals to date, including endorsements, autograph signings, and personal appearances.

Other Men's Sports
For athletes in sports with less exposure, such as baseball, wrestling, or track and field, the opportunities to monetize their NIL might be fewer and smaller in scale. However, these athletes can still benefit from NIL policies by leveraging their personal brand within their community, local businesses, or specific niches related to their sport. Additionally, opportunities for monetizing social media platforms or running private camps or clinics can apply to athletes in any sport.

Women's Sports
The advent of NIL rights has been particularly impactful for women's sports. Despite typically receiving less media attention than men's football and basketball, several female athletes have substantial social media followings and have been successful in securing endorsement deals. There has been an increase in gymnast's popularity on social media, for example, where some individual student-athletes can garner millions of social media followers and therefore are positioned to be among the top earners in the NIL era.

Non-Revenue Sports
For athletes in non-revenue sports (those that typically do not generate a significant profit for universities), NIL opens up a new avenue for financial opportunities. While the deals may not be as lucrative as those for high-profile sports, athletes could still form partnerships with local businesses, monetize their social media platforms, and offer private lessons or clinics, among other possibilities.

Equity and Inclusion
It's important to note that while NIL presents exciting opportunities, it also raises

questions about equity. High-profile athletes in popular sports stand to make significantly more than their peers in less popular sports. Similarly, athletes with larger social media followings or more marketable personas may have more opportunities. As NIL policies continue to evolve, it will be important for regulators and universities to consider how to promote fairness and inclusion across all sports.

VIII. NIL Representatives, Sports Agents, and Ethical Considerations

The Name, Image, and Likeness (NIL) era introduces an intriguing dynamic between NIL representatives and traditional sports agents. These two roles, while distinct in their purposes and regulations, may overlap and interact in ways that raise ethical and legal questions.

The Interplay Between NIL Representatives and Sports Agents
NIL representatives focus solely on assisting student-athletes with opportunities to monetize their NIL rights while they are in college. Their activities may include securing endorsement deals, negotiating contracts, and providing guidance on branding and marketing.

Sports agents, on the other hand, traditionally represent athletes in negotiations for professional contracts and endorsement deals post-college. They may also provide career management and financial advice.
Given the potential for significant income from NIL deals, some sports agents might be inclined to offer NIL representation services in an effort to build relationships with athletes early on. When the student-athlete's NCAA eligibility expires, these agents could potentially transition into a traditional sports agent role, providing a smooth path from collegiate to professional representation.

Ethical Concerns
This intersection of roles presents a host of potential ethical concerns. The foremost being the question of whether it's appropriate or fair for sports agents to use NIL representation as a way to "recruit" future clients while they are still college athletes. Critics argue that this could potentially exploit student-athletes and detract from their educational and sporting commitments.

Secondly, there's a risk of conflict of interest. Agents who are also acting as NIL representatives may be tempted to prioritize their own long-term interests (securing a future professional client) over the immediate best interests of the student-athlete in their NIL activities.

Regulatory Safeguards
To mitigate these concerns, the NCAA has also stipulated that student-athletes who engage an agent for NIL purposes must ensure that the agreement doesn't conflict with NCAA rules. For example, the agent cannot arrange for future professional sports opportunities or promise future professional representation as part of the NIL agreement.

Outlook

While the NIL era opens up new avenues for student-athletes, it also creates new challenges and ethical considerations. Balancing the interests of student-athletes with those of NIL representatives and sports agents will be an ongoing task. It's critical that all parties navigate this dynamic responsibly, always prioritizing the best interests of the student-athletes. The regulatory landscape, which continues to evolve, will play a crucial role in ensuring that this new era is not just prosperous, but also fair and ethical.

IX. Current Trends

The dawn of Name, Image, and Likeness (NIL) rights for NCAA student-athletes has given rise to a number of key trends:

1. The Rise of Personal Brands and Entrepreneurship: Student-athletes are not just seen as individuals but as brands in their own right. This perspective has encouraged entrepreneurial activities, such as the development of their own merchandise lines, paid appearances, or the creation of personal fitness and training programs.

2. Monetizing Social Media Platforms: In the age of digital technology, social media platforms have become a significant avenue for athletes to monetize their NIL rights. The use of sponsored posts, advertisements, and collaborations with digital brands has gained traction, as athletes leverage their online followings to generate income.

3. The Emergence of Collectives and Pooled Sponsorship: This is a novel concept in which athletes band together to negotiate deals and endorsements. Pooled sponsorship agreements provide a framework for companies to work with entire teams or specific groups of athletes, which can be more attractive for sponsors looking for wider reach and impact.

4. Partnerships with Third-Party Companies: As the NIL space is complex and often challenging to navigate, athletes and universities are leaning on third-party firms for support. These companies offer services such as contract negotiation, compliance checks, financial management education, and brand development.

5. Emphasis on Financial Literacy: The potential influx of income for student-athletes has underscored the importance of financial literacy. Universities, often in partnership with third-party firms, are implementing programs to equip athletes with the knowledge to manage their finances effectively.

6. Inclusive Opportunities Across Sports and Genders: The opportunities provided by NIL are not restricted to male athletes or the most popular sports. Athletes from a wide range of sports and female athletes have been successful in leveraging their NIL rights, illustrating the broad scope of these new opportunities.

These trends underscore the evolving dynamics of collegiate sports in the NIL era. As the landscape continues to shift, these trends may change and new ones may emerge, shaping the future trajectory of student-athlete compensation and collegiate sports.

X. Future Predictions

As we navigate through the early stages of the Name, Image, and Likeness (NIL) era, the future still holds many unknowns. Nevertheless, several predictions can be made based on the trends and patterns that have emerged so far.

1. Increased Professionalization of College Sports: The introduction of NIL rights has blurred the lines between amateurism and professionalism in collegiate sports. We can expect this shift to continue, with athletes increasingly being seen as individual brands and businesses.

2. Continued Regulatory Evolution: The current landscape of state laws and NCAA regulations is likely to continue to evolve as issues arise and stakeholders gain more understanding of the implications of NIL rights. Federal legislation, which would provide a nationwide standard, could also be on the horizon.

3. Greater Emphasis on Financial Literacy and Support Services: As student-athletes begin to navigate the complexities of contracts, tax implications, and financial management, universities and third parties will likely expand resources and services to support these athletes.

4. Increased Competition Among Universities: Universities' approaches to NIL will become an increasingly important factor in recruiting top talent. As a result, we can expect universities to continue to expand their NIL-related offerings, from educational programs to partnerships with brand management companies.

5. Expanding Market for NIL-related Services: As student-athletes seek to monetize their NIL rights, the market for related services will continue to grow. Companies offering services such as brand management, contract negotiation, and financial planning are poised to benefit.

6. Innovative NIL Opportunities: As the NIL marketplace matures, we'll likely see the emergence of more creative and innovative ways for student-athletes to monetize their NIL, from unique partnerships and sponsorships to new entrepreneurial endeavors.

7. Equity Challenges: As NIL opportunities continue to grow, issues of equity among athletes from different sports, backgrounds, and genders

will likely become a focal point of discussions. Strategies for maintaining fair opportunities for all student-athletes will need to be developed.

These predictions highlight the transformative potential that NIL has for the future of collegiate sports. As the landscape continues to evolve, stakeholders must continue to adapt and respond to ensure the best outcomes for all involved.

XI. NIL and tax

The NCAA's recent decision to permit student-athletes to benefit from their Name, Image, and Likeness (NIL) represents a monumental shift in the realm of college sports. This development ushers in a new era where student-athletes can monetize their NIL rights, engage with businesses, and enter into endorsement contracts, all while maintaining their amateur status. However, with these newfound opportunities come significant tax implications that may be unfamiliar to these young athletes and the collectives they are part of.

The IRS has clear guidelines that stipulate any income earned, whether through employment or otherwise, is subject to federal income tax. Thus, NIL earnings from endorsements, social media promotions, merchandise sales, or personal appearances are considered taxable income. Athletes will need to report this income on their annual tax returns. Depending on their earnings, they could potentially be pushed into higher tax brackets, resulting in a significant tax liability. This aspect can be challenging to navigate, especially for student-athletes who might not be well-versed in handling complex tax issues.

State tax implications must also be considered. Depending on where the student-athlete resides or where their income is earned, they might be subject to state income tax. This could complicate matters further for those participating in interstate competitions or promotional events. Moreover, many states have different rules for what is considered taxable, leading to potential discrepancies between state and federal tax obligations.

For international student-athletes, the situation could be even more complex. They may be subject to tax both in the US and their home countries, depending on various tax treaties and their particular international tax situations. It is essential that these student-athletes obtain appropriate tax advice to ensure they meet their obligations and don't incur unnecessary liabilities.

Collectives – organizations established by student-athletes pooling their NIL rights – are also subject to tax implications. If operated as a business, collectives would typically be subject to corporate tax on their earnings. If the collective decides to distribute earnings to members (the student-athletes), these would then be classified as personal income for the athletes and taxed accordingly.

Moreover, the establishment of a collective may trigger Unrelated Business Income Tax (UBIT) considerations. For example, if a tax-exempt entity, such as a university, is deemed to have an ownership interest or control in a collective, the income derived from the collective's activities could potentially be subject to UBIT.

It's important to note that certain deductions may be available to offset some of these tax burdens. For instance, expenses directly related to earning NIL income, like travel for promotional appearances or fees for agents or tax advisors, may be deductible. Similarly, collectives operating as businesses may be able to claim business-related expenses.

As we navigate this new landscape, it's crucial for student-athletes, and the collectives they're part of, to understand the tax implications of their NIL activities. The potential for significant income brings the need for financial literacy, responsible money management, and appropriate tax planning. Universities, compliance officers, and athletic departments should prioritize education on these issues to prepare their student-athletes for this new reality. It's a brave new world in college sports, and with the right knowledge and advice, student-athletes can fully embrace their NIL opportunities while also being financially savvy.

While the NIL rights of student-athletes bring newfound financial opportunities, they also introduce a new layer of complexity to their financial lives. It's crucial to ensure these young people are equipped with the understanding and resources they need to navigate this complexity, ensuring that today's opportunities don't become tomorrow's liabilities.

XII. Conclusion

The advent of Name, Image, and Likeness (NIL) rights for NCAA student-athletes has ushered in a new era in collegiate sports. With a dynamic mix of opportunities and challenges, the NIL landscape is transforming the collegiate sports ecosystem, reshaping the student-athlete experience, and redefining the boundaries of amateurism.
It's a time of significant change, where the intersection of sports, business, and law is more visible and complex than ever before. From the shifting regulatory landscape to the evolving economic opportunities and implications for student-athletes, the impact of NIL rights is broad and far-reaching.

Universities, student-athletes, businesses, and regulators must navigate this new terrain with care and diligence, balancing the opportunities it presents with the potential risks and challenges it carries. In doing so, the focus should always remain on the well-being and fair treatment of student-athletes.

As we move forward in the NIL era, continued learning, adaptability, and collaboration will be key. The journey is just beginning, and the road ahead is sure to bring more changes, surprises, and opportunities for growth.

The potential of NIL rights extends beyond the monetary gains for student-athletes. It's a catalyst for change, spurring discussions on equity, pushing for financial literacy, and prompting the reassessment of long-standing notions of amateurism. In this sense, the NIL revolution is more than just a change in rules – it's a critical step forward in the evolution of collegiate sports.

About the author:

Tanner Simkins is founder and CEO of Complete SET Agency, a full service sports entertainment firm that works with brands, athletes and entertainers. As an author, Tanner shares his expertise through his 15 year career as sports agent and award-winning business owner. Simkins holds degrees from University of Miami and Columbia University.

www.ingramcontent.com/pod-product-compliance
Lightning Source LLC
Chambersburg PA
CBHW081136170426
43197CB00017B/2884